Ludlow
Travel Guide 2024

Medieval Magic in
Shropshire

Desiree M. Dominion

Table of contents

Conclusion and Final Tips for a Memorable Trip

Introduction

Welcome to Ludlow, a picturesque town nestled in the heart of England, where history, charm, and natural beauty seamlessly converge. This mediaeval market town, situated in Shropshire, boasts a rich tapestry of architectural heritage, with its timber-framed buildings, cobbled streets, and a majestic castle that stands as a testament to centuries gone by.

Ludlow's enchanting streets invite you to wander through its vibrant marketplaces, where local vendors offer a delightful array of fresh produce, artisan crafts, and culinary delights. Renowned for its gastronomic scene, Ludlow is a haven for food enthusiasts, hosting an annual Food Festival that attracts chefs, producers, and food lovers from far and wide.

Beyond the culinary delights, Ludlow's historical significance is evident in landmarks like Ludlow Castle, a Norman fortress that has witnessed centuries of events. The castle's commanding presence provides a captivating backdrop to the town, and visitors can explore its grounds, immersing themselves in tales of battles and royal intrigue.

Surrounded by the lush Shropshire Hills, Ludlow is a gateway to the stunning countryside, offering scenic walks and outdoor adventures. The River Teme meanders through the landscape, providing a tranquil setting for riverside strolls and picturesque views.

Whether you're captivated by history, enticed by culinary wonders, or seeking the tranquillity of nature, Ludlow beckons with open arms. Join us on a journey through this charming town, where every cobblestone tells a story, and every corner reveals a piece of England's past.

Brief History of Ludlow

Nestled along the meandering River Teme in Shropshire, England, Ludlow stands as a testament to centuries of history and cultural richness. Surrounded by lush greenery and picturesque landscapes, the town provides a tranquil escape from the hustle and bustle of modern life.

Historic Charm:

At the heart of Ludlow lies the imposing Ludlow Castle, a mediaeval fortress that dominates the skyline. Built in the 11th century, the castle offers a glimpse into the town's storied past and serves as a venue for events and festivals. The cobbled streets are lined with timber-framed buildings, showcasing Tudor and Georgian architecture, creating an atmosphere reminiscent of a bygone era.

Cultural Hub:

Ludlow is a cultural hub with a vibrant arts scene. The town hosts various events throughout the year, from classical music concerts to lively festivals celebrating literature and the arts. Visitors can explore the Ludlow Assembly Rooms, a cultural centre that often features theatrical performances, film screenings, and art exhibitions.

Gastronomic Paradise:

Renowned as a food lover's paradise, Ludlow boasts a gastronomic scene that has earned it the title of "The Foodie Town." The bustling market, held within the mediaeval walls, showcases local produce, artisanal crafts, and delectable treats. Ludlow's restaurants and pubs are celebrated for their commitment to using locally sourced ingredients, creating a culinary experience that reflects the region's flavours.

Scenic Surroundings:
Beyond the town's borders, Ludlow is surrounded by the serene Shropshire countryside. Hiking trails, such as the Mortimer Trail and the Shropshire Way, offer breathtaking views of rolling hills and picturesque landscapes. Ludlow's proximity to the Shropshire Hills Area of Outstanding Natural Beauty adds to the allure for nature enthusiasts.

Community Spirit:
Ludlow exudes a strong sense of community, with locals passionate about preserving the town's heritage and fostering a welcoming atmosphere. Events like the Ludlow Food Festival and Ludlow Medieval Christmas Fayre bring residents and visitors together, creating a lively and inclusive environment.

In essence, Ludlow is a town that seamlessly blends its historical roots with a contemporary flair, offering a multifaceted experience for those seeking cultural richness, culinary delights, and the beauty of the English countryside.

Geography and Climate

Geography:
Ludlow is situated in the county of Shropshire, in the West Midlands region of England. The town is strategically located along the River Teme, providing a scenic setting with its bridges and riverside views. Surrounded by undulating hills and green landscapes, Ludlow is part of the Shropshire Hills Area of Outstanding Natural Beauty, contributing to its overall charm and appeal.

Climate:
Ludlow experiences a temperate maritime climate, typical of much of the United Kingdom. The town enjoys mild temperatures, with relatively cool winters and warm summers. Here's a breakdown of the seasons:

Winter (December to February): Winter temperatures in Ludlow typically range from 2 to 8 degrees Celsius (36 to 46 degrees

Fahrenheit). While it can get chilly, snowfall is generally moderate, and the town takes on a serene, festive atmosphere.

Spring (March to May): Spring brings milder temperatures, with averages ranging from 6 to 14 degrees Celsius (43 to 57 degrees Fahrenheit). The surrounding countryside comes to life with blossoming flowers, adding to Ludlow's picturesque appeal.

Summer (June to August): Ludlow experiences pleasant summers, with temperatures averaging between 14 and 21 degrees Celsius (57 to 70 degrees Fahrenheit). The longer days invite outdoor activities, and the town's greenery is at its vibrant best.

Autumn (September to November): Autumn in Ludlow sees temperatures gradually cooling, ranging from 7 to 14 degrees Celsius (45 to 57 degrees Fahrenheit). The surrounding hills adorned with autumnal colours create a scenic backdrop for visitors.

Rainfall is evenly distributed throughout the year, and Ludlow benefits from its proximity to the Welsh border, which can influence weather patterns. The town's climate contributes to its lush landscapes and makes it an inviting destination for those seeking a balance between historical exploration and natural beauty

Why Visit Ludlow

Ludlow beckons travellers for a myriad of compelling reasons, creating a tapestry of experiences that make it a must-visit destination.

Historical Marvels: Ludlow's mediaeval heritage is palpable as you stroll through its well-preserved streets. Ludlow Castle, dating back to the 11th century, stands as a testament to the town's historical significance. Explore the castle's towers, ramparts, and mediaeval rooms to transport yourself back in time.

Culinary Delights: Ludlow is a culinary haven, earning its place as a designated "Food Town." The town's renowned Food Festival attracts gastronomy enthusiasts from near and far. Immerse yourself in a world of artisanal cheeses, locally sourced produce, and delectable dishes crafted by talented chefs. Ludlow's diverse range of eateries, from traditional pubs to fine dining establishments, ensures a delightful gastronomic adventure.

Quaint Market Town Atmosphere: Ludlow's charm lies in its market town ambiance. Traverse cobbled streets lined with independent shops, boutiques, and galleries. The vibrant marketplaces offer a chance to interact with friendly locals and discover unique treasures, from handmade crafts to vintage finds.

Natural Beauty: Set against the backdrop of the Shropshire Hills, Ludlow is surrounded by picturesque landscapes. Nature enthusiasts can explore scenic walking trails, meander along the River Teme, or simply bask in the tranquillity of the countryside. The Ludlow Food Centre is not only a culinary delight but also set in beautiful surroundings, showcasing the region's natural bounty.

Arts and Culture: Ludlow is a hub for arts and culture, hosting events, festivals, and performances throughout the year. The Assembly Rooms and Ludlow Fringe Festival provide platforms for artists, musicians, and performers, creating a vibrant cultural scene that enriches the town's atmosphere.

Friendly Community: Ludlow's welcoming community adds an extra layer of warmth to your visit. Whether engaging with locals at the market or enjoying a conversation in one of the charming pubs, the friendly spirit of Ludlow enhances the overall experience.

In essence, Ludlow offers a harmonious blend of history, gastronomy, natural beauty, and cultural vibrancy. Whether you seek a tranquil retreat, a culinary adventure, or a journey through mediaeval history, Ludlow invites you to indulge in an enriching and unforgettable experience

Chapter One: Getting Started

Planning Your Trip

Planning a trip to Ludlow involves considering various aspects to ensure a smooth and enjoyable experience. Here's a detailed guide:

Research Ludlow:
Explore Ludlow's history, attractions, and culture.
Identify key landmarks, museums, and outdoor activities.

Set Travel Dates:
Check the weather for your preferred travel time.
Consider any local events or festivals that might influence your visit.

Accommodation:
Look for hotels, bed and breakfasts, or vacation rentals.
Consider proximity to attractions and read reviews for informed choices.

Transportation:

When planning a trip to Ludlow, visitors should choose the most suitable transportation option for their needs, whether it be by car, train, or bus.

If driving, plan your route and parking options.

Create Itinerary:
Outline a daily schedule with activities and meals.
Include flexibility for spontaneous discoveries.

Local Cuisine:
Research local restaurants and specialties.
Consider making reservations for popular places.

Budgeting:
Estimate costs for accommodation, transportation, meals, and activities.
Set aside extra funds for unexpected expenses.

Packing:
Check the weather forecast and pack accordingly.

Make sure to bring essential items such as chargers, medications, and travel documents when planning your trip to Ludlow.

Attractions and Activities:
Prioritise attractions based on personal interests.
Check opening hours and any admission fees.

Local Etiquette:
Learn about local customs and etiquette.
Respect cultural norms and engage with locals respectfully.

Safety Precautions:
familiarise yourself with emergency contacts and medical facilities.
Keep a copy of important documents, such as ID and travel insurance.

Communication:
Check mobile network coverage and data plans.
Learn a few basic local phrases for communication.

Photography:
Research photography rules at various attractions.

Bring necessary equipment and extra memory cards.

Connect with Locals:
Join local events or tours for an authentic experience.
Use social media or travel forums to get tips from residents.

Final Check:
Confirm reservations and transportation details.
Additionally, consider sharing your itinerary with a friend or family member.

By planning comprehensively, you'll be better prepared to make the most of your trip to Ludlow. Safe travels.

Best Time to Visit

Ludlow, a quaint market town located in Shropshire, England, is a charming destination that attracts visitors year-round. However, the best time to visit Ludlow largely depends on individual preferences and interests.

Spring is a popular time to visit Ludlow, as the town comes alive with vibrant blooms and blossoming trees. The surrounding countryside is lush and green, making it an ideal time for outdoor activities such as hiking, cycling, and picnicking. The annual Ludlow Spring Festival, held in May, is a major draw for food and drink enthusiasts, featuring a wide array of local produce, artisanal foods, and craft beers.

Summer is another excellent time to visit Ludlow, as the weather is warm and sunny, making it perfect for exploring the town's historic streets and landmarks. The Ludlow Fringe Festival, which takes place in June and July, offers a diverse range of performances, including music, comedy, theatre, and art exhibitions. Additionally, the Ludlow Food Festival in September is a must-visit for foodies, showcasing the best of local and regional food and drink.

Autumn is a beautiful time to visit Ludlow, as the surrounding countryside is adorned with stunning fall foliage. The town's annual Medieval Christmas Fayre in November is a festive event that transports visitors back in time with its traditional market stalls, live entertainment, and historical reenactments.

Winter in Ludlow is a magical time, with the town adorned with festive decorations and twinkling lights. The Ludlow Medieval Christmas Fayre continues into December, offering a unique opportunity to experience a traditional Christmas market in a historic setting. Additionally, Ludlow's annual Christmas Lights Switch On event brings the community together for a festive celebration.

Ultimately, the best time to visit Ludlow depends on individual interests and what one hopes to experience during their visit. Whether it's enjoying the beauty of spring blooms, indulging in culinary delights at a food festival, or immersing oneself in the festive spirit during the holiday season, Ludlow offers something special year-round.

Transportation Options

Ludlow offers a variety of transportation options for visitors to explore the town and its surrounding areas. The town is easily accessible by car, with several major roads connecting it to nearby cities such as Shrewsbury, Hereford, and Worcester. There are also ample parking facilities available in and around the town centre for those travelling by car.

For those who prefer to use public transportation, Ludlow is served by a local bus service that connects the town to neighbouring villages and towns. The Ludlow Park and Ride service also provides a convenient option for visitors to leave their cars on the outskirts of town and take a bus into the centre, reducing traffic congestion in the town centre.

Additionally, Ludlow has a train station located just a short walk from the town centre, offering regular services to destinations such as Shrewsbury, Hereford, and Cardiff. The train station provides easy access for visitors arriving by train and is a convenient option for exploring the surrounding area without the need for a car.

For those who prefer to explore the town on foot or by bicycle, Ludlow offers a network of pedestrian-friendly streets and pathways, making it easy to navigate the town centre and enjoy its historic charm. There are also several bicycle rental shops in Ludlow, providing an eco-friendly and active way to explore the town and its picturesque countryside.

Overall, Ludlow provides a range of transportation options to suit the needs of visitors, whether they prefer to drive, take public transportation, or explore the town on foot or by bicycle. This accessibility makes it easy for visitors to experience all that Ludlow has to offer, from its historic landmarks and charming streets to its vibrant festivals and natural beauty.

Chapter Two: Explore Ludlow

Main Attractions

Ludlow, is a popular destination for visitors seeking to explore its rich history, stunning architecture, and vibrant cultural scene. One of the main attractions in Ludlow is its historic Ludlow Castle, which dates back to the 11th century and offers a fascinating glimpse into the town's mediaeval past. The castle's impressive ruins, towers, and ramparts provide a striking backdrop for events such as the Ludlow Food and Drink Festival, as well as offering visitors the chance to explore its grounds and enjoy panoramic views of the surrounding countryside.

In addition to Ludlow Castle, the town is home to a number of other historic landmarks, including St. Laurence's Church, known for its stunning architecture and beautiful stained glass windows. The town's mediaeval streets are lined with charming timber-framed buildings, many of which now house independent shops, art galleries, and traditional pubs, making it a delight to explore on foot.

Ludlow is also renowned for its thriving food scene, with a wide range of restaurants, cafes, and food shops offering delicious local produce and culinary delights. The Ludlow Food Centre, located just outside of town, is a must-visit for food enthusiasts, as it showcases the best of Shropshire's artisanal cheeses, meats, baked goods, and more.

For those interested in the arts, Ludlow has several galleries and performance spaces, including the Ludlow Assembly Rooms, which hosts a diverse program of live music, theatre, and film screenings throughout the year. The town also plays host to various festivals and events, such as the Ludlow Fringe Festival and the Ludlow Medieval Christmas Fayre, which offer unique opportunities to experience the town's vibrant cultural scene.

Outdoor enthusiasts will find plenty to enjoy in Ludlow's surrounding countryside, with numerous walking trails, cycling routes, and nature reserves to explore. The Shropshire Hills Area of Outstanding Natural Beauty is also within easy reach, offering breathtaking landscapes and outdoor activities such as hiking, birdwatching, and wildlife spotting.

Overall, Ludlow offers a wealth of attractions for visitors to enjoy, from its historic landmarks and cultural offerings to its stunning natural surroundings and delicious local food and drink. Whether exploring the town's mediaeval heritage or immersing oneself in its vibrant arts and culinary scene, Ludlow has something to offer every type of traveller.

Ludlow Castle

Ludlow Castle is a historic landmark located in the town of Ludlow, Shropshire, England. It is a mediaeval fortress that dates back to the 11th century and has a rich history as a royal residence, military stronghold, and centre of government.

The castle is known for its impressive architecture, including its imposing walls, towers, and gatehouse. Visitors can explore the various parts of the castle, including the Great Hall, the Chapel, and the living quarters. The castle also offers stunning views of the surrounding countryside from its battlements.

In addition to its architectural significance, Ludlow Castle has played a significant role in English history. It was the seat of power for the Council of the Marches, which governed the border region between England and Wales. The castle has also been the site of important historical events, including battles and political intrigue.

Today, Ludlow Castle is a popular tourist attraction, offering guided tours, events, and activities for visitors of all ages. The castle hosts a variety of events throughout the year, including historical reenactments, concerts, and festivals.

Visitors to Ludlow Castle can also enjoy the surrounding town of Ludlow, which is known for its charming streets, historic buildings, and vibrant food scene. The town is home to a variety of shops, restaurants, and accommodations, making it a great destination for a day trip or a longer stay.

Overall, Ludlow Castle is a must-see destination for history enthusiasts, architecture lovers, and anyone looking to immerse themselves in the rich heritage of England. Whether you're interested in exploring mediaeval fortresses or simply enjoying the picturesque surroundings, Ludlow Castle has something to offer for every traveller.

St. Laurence's Church

St. Laurence's Church is a historic church located in the town of Ludlow, Shropshire, England, and is situated near Ludlow Castle. The church has a rich history dating back to the 12th century and is known for its impressive architecture and significant role in the community.

The church's architecture is a mix of styles, including Norman, Gothic, and Victorian, reflecting its long history of construction and renovation. The church features a striking tower, stained glass windows, and intricate stone carvings, making it a notable example of mediaeval and later English religious architecture.

St. Laurence's Church has played an important role in the religious and social life of Ludlow. It has been a place of worship, community gatherings, and cultural events for centuries. The church has also been the site of important historical events, including royal visits and religious ceremonies.

Visitors to St. Laurence's Church can explore its interior, which features beautiful vaulted ceilings, ornate furnishings, and historic monuments. The church also offers guided tours and hosts regular services, concerts, and other events for the local community and visitors.

In addition to its architectural and historical significance, St. Laurence's Church is known for its vibrant community and commitment to preserving its heritage. The church is actively involved in local outreach and charitable work, making it an integral part of Ludlow's social fabric.

Overall, St. Laurence's Church is a must-see destination for anyone interested in history, architecture, or religious heritage. Whether you're exploring Ludlow Castle or simply taking in the town's historic sites, a visit to St. Laurence's Church offers a unique opportunity to immerse yourself in the rich history and culture of this charming English town.

Ludlow Food and Drink Festival

The Ludlow Food and Drink Festival is an annual event held in the town of Ludlow, Shropshire, England, and is a celebration of the region's culinary heritage and local produce. The festival has been running for over 20 years and has become a popular attraction for food enthusiasts and visitors from around the country.

The festival takes place in the historic setting of Ludlow Castle, providing a picturesque backdrop for the event. It typically spans over a weekend and features a wide range of activities, including food and drink stalls, cooking demonstrations, tastings, and live entertainment.

One of the main highlights of the Ludlow Food and Drink Festival is the abundance of local and regional food and drink producers who showcase their products at the event. Visitors have the opportunity to sample and purchase a variety of artisanal cheeses, meats, baked goods, preserves, and beverages, all of which are made using traditional methods and high-quality ingredients.

In addition to the food and drink stalls, the festival also hosts cooking demonstrations by renowned chefs and culinary experts. These demonstrations provide insight into different cooking techniques, recipes, and the use of local ingredients, offering visitors a chance to learn from professionals and expand their culinary skills.

Live entertainment is another key feature of the Ludlow Food and Drink Festival, with music performances, street performers, and family-friendly activities adding to the festive atmosphere. The event often includes workshops, talks, and tastings focused on specific food and drink themes, such as wine pairing, cheese making, or foraging.

The Ludlow Food and Drink Festival is also committed to promoting sustainable and ethical food practices, with a focus on supporting local farmers, producers, and businesses. Many of the vendors at the festival emphasise the use of organic, seasonal, and locally sourced ingredients, contributing to the region's reputation for high-quality and environmentally conscious food production.

Overall, the Ludlow Food and Drink Festival offers a unique opportunity for visitors to experience the rich culinary traditions of Shropshire and the surrounding areas. With its diverse range of activities, delicious offerings, and vibrant atmosphere, the festival has become a beloved annual event that showcases the best of local food and drink culture.

Hidden Treasures

While Ludlow's historic castle and beautiful church are well-known attractions, the town also boasts a number of hidden treasures waiting to be discovered by visitors.

One such hidden treasure is the Ludlow Museum, located in the heart of the town. Housed in a charming timber-framed building, the museum offers a fascinating insight into Ludlow's history, with displays covering everything from the town's mediaeval origins to its more recent industrial past. Visitors can explore artefacts, photographs, and interactive exhibits that bring the town's heritage to life, making it a must-visit for history enthusiasts.

Another hidden treasure in Ludlow is the Buttercross, a striking 18th-century market hall located in the town centre. This elegant structure, with its distinctive clock tower and open arches, has been a focal point of Ludlow's market square for centuries and is a wonderful example of Georgian architecture. The Buttercross is still used as a market space today, hosting regular markets and events, and is a delightful spot to soak up the town's bustling atmosphere.

For those interested in horticulture and natural beauty, the walled gardens at Stokesay Court offer a peaceful retreat just a short drive from Ludlow. These stunning gardens, which have been lovingly restored in recent years, feature a variety of rare and exotic plants, as well as beautifully landscaped lawns, ponds, and pathways. Visitors can take a leisurely stroll through the gardens, admiring the colourful blooms and tranquil surroundings, making it a perfect spot for a relaxing afternoon.

Ludlow is also home to a number of hidden alleyways and courtyards, which are filled with character and charm. These secluded spots are often home to independent shops, artisan workshops, and cosy cafes, offering a chance to escape the hustle and bustle of the main streets and discover unique treasures off the beaten path.

Overall, Ludlow's hidden treasures offer visitors the opportunity to delve deeper into the town's history, culture, and natural beauty, uncovering unique experiences and attractions that add an extra layer of richness to a visit to this delightful market town.

Ludlow Museum

The Ludlow Museum is a hidden treasure located in the heart of Ludlow, offering visitors a fascinating glimpse into the town's rich history. Housed in a charming timber-framed building, the museum is a must-visit for history enthusiasts and anyone looking to delve deeper into Ludlow's past.

The museum's exhibits cover a wide range of topics, from the town's mediaeval origins to its more recent industrial history. Visitors can explore a diverse collection of artefacts, photographs, and interactive displays that bring Ludlow's heritage to life. The museum provides a comprehensive overview of the town's development, making it a valuable resource for those interested in learning about Ludlow's cultural and historical significance.

One of the highlights of the museum is its collection of mediaeval artefacts, including pottery, tools, and household items that offer a fascinating insight into daily life in Ludlow during this period. The museum also showcases the town's industrial heritage, with displays on traditional crafts and industries that once thrived in Ludlow.

In addition to its permanent exhibits, the Ludlow Museum also hosts temporary displays and special events throughout the year, ensuring that there is always something new to discover for returning visitors.

The museum is staffed by knowledgeable and friendly volunteers who are passionate about sharing Ludlow's history with visitors. They are on hand to answer questions and provide additional information about the exhibits, adding an extra layer of depth to the visitor experience.

Overall, the Ludlow Museum is a hidden treasure that offers a unique and immersive way to explore the town's history and culture. Whether you're a history enthusiast or simply curious about Ludlow's past, a visit to the museum is sure to enrich your understanding of this charming market town.

The Feathers Hotel

The Feathers Hotel is a historic and iconic attraction in Ludlow, offering visitors a luxurious and unforgettable experience in the heart of the town. This stunning hotel is renowned for its distinctive half-timbered facade, which dates back to the 17th century and exudes charm and character.

The Feathers Hotel boasts a rich history, having been a prominent coaching inn during the heyday of travel in England. Today, the hotel seamlessly combines its heritage with modern amenities, providing guests with a comfortable and elegant stay. The interior of the hotel is adorned with exquisite period features, including oak panelling, antique furniture, and ornate fireplaces, creating a truly enchanting atmosphere.

In addition to its beautiful accommodations, The Feathers Hotel is also home to a renowned restaurant that offers a fine dining experience. Guests can indulge in delectable cuisine made from locally sourced ingredients, accompanied by an extensive selection of wines and spirits. The hotel's restaurant provides a sophisticated setting for a memorable meal, whether it's a romantic dinner or a celebratory gathering.

The Feathers Hotel is also a popular venue for special events and celebrations, such as weddings, private parties, and corporate functions. The hotel's elegant function rooms and attentive staff ensure that every event is executed with precision and style, making it a sought-after destination for those looking to host a memorable occasion.

Furthermore, The Feathers Hotel is ideally situated for exploring Ludlow's attractions, including its historic castle, vibrant market, and independent shops. Its central location allows guests to immerse themselves in the town's rich heritage and lively atmosphere, making it an ideal base for discovering all that Ludlow has to offer.

Overall, The Feathers Hotel is a standout attraction in Ludlow, offering a blend of history, luxury, and hospitality that captivates visitors and leaves a lasting impression. Whether staying overnight or simply enjoying a meal or drink, a visit to this historic hotel is sure to be a highlight of any trip to Ludlow.

Ludlow Assembly Rooms

The Ludlow Assembly Rooms is a vibrant and dynamic cultural attraction in the heart of

Ludlow, offering a diverse range of entertainment and events for visitors to enjoy. This historic building has been a hub of creativity and community for over 200 years, and continues to be a focal point for the arts in the town.

The Ludlow Assembly Rooms hosts a wide variety of performances, including live music, theatre productions, comedy shows, and dance performances. Its versatile spaces, including a main auditorium and smaller studio spaces, allow for a diverse program of events that cater to all tastes and interests. Whether it's a classic play, a contemporary concert, or a family-friendly show, there's always something exciting happening at the Assembly Rooms.

In addition to its live performances, the Ludlow Assembly Rooms also screens a selection of films, from independent and foreign movies to popular blockbusters. Its cinema program offers a unique and intimate setting for film enthusiasts to enjoy the latest releases and timeless classics alike.

Furthermore, the Assembly Rooms is home to a bustling cafe and bar, providing a welcoming space for visitors to relax and socialise before or after a performance. The cafe offers a tempting selection of hot and cold drinks, as well as light bites and sweet treats, making it a popular spot for locals and tourists alike.

The Ludlow Assembly Rooms also plays an important role in the community, hosting workshops, classes, and educational programs for people of all ages. From art and craft sessions to dance and drama workshops, the venue offers opportunities for creativity and learning that enrich the lives of those in Ludlow and beyond.

Overall, the Ludlow Assembly Rooms is a must-visit attraction for anyone looking to immerse themselves in the cultural life of the town. With its diverse program of events, welcoming atmosphere, and commitment to community engagement, it's a place where creativity thrives and unforgettable experiences are made.

Chapter Three: Accommodations

Hotels

Ludlow, is home to a variety of charming and comfortable hotels that cater to the needs of visitors looking for a relaxing and enjoyable stay. From historic coaching inns to boutique hotels, Ludlow offers accommodation options to suit every taste and budget.

One of the most renowned hotels in Ludlow is the Feathers Hotel, a historic coaching inn that dates back to the 17th century. This elegant hotel boasts a rich history and a prime location in the heart of the town, making it a popular choice for travellers. The Feathers Hotel offers a range of beautifully decorated rooms, some of which feature four-poster beds and antique furnishings. Guests can also enjoy fine dining at the hotel's award-winning restaurant, as well as a cosy bar and lounge area.

For those seeking a more contemporary and stylish accommodation option, the Ludlow Mascall Centre is a modern hotel located in a stunning Georgian building. The hotel offers comfortable and well-appointed rooms, as well as excellent amenities including a restaurant, bar, and beautiful garden grounds. The Ludlow Mascall Centre is perfect for travellers looking for a peaceful and tranquil retreat in Ludlow.

Additionally, the Castle Hotel is another popular choice for visitors to Ludlow. This boutique hotel is situated within a historic building and offers a blend of traditional charm and modern comfort. The Castle Hotel features individually designed rooms, a cosy bar and lounge area, and an acclaimed restaurant serving delicious meals made with locally sourced ingredients.

For those seeking a more budget-friendly option, Ludlow also offers a selection of bed and breakfast establishments and guesthouses that provide comfortable accommodation and warm hospitality. These smaller establishments often offer personalised service and a homely atmosphere, making them an excellent choice for travellers looking for a more intimate and authentic experience.

Overall, Ludlow's hotels cater to a range of preferences and provide visitors with the perfect base from which to explore the town's historic attractions, cultural events, and natural beauty. Whether it's a luxury stay at a historic inn or a cosy bed and breakfast, Ludlow's hotels offer something for everyone.

Bed and Breakfasts

Ludlow offers a selection of charming and cosy bed and breakfast establishments that provide visitors with a warm and welcoming stay. One popular choice is The Graig Bed and Breakfast, a beautiful Victorian property located just a short walk from the town centre. This family-run B&B offers comfortable and tastefully decorated rooms, a delicious breakfast served in a bright dining room, and a peaceful garden area for guests to relax in.

Another well-regarded bed and breakfast in Ludlow is Elm Lodge Bed and Breakfast, a lovely Edwardian house situated in a quiet residential area. This B&B provides comfortable and spacious rooms, a hearty breakfast featuring locally sourced produce, and a friendly and attentive host who is happy to offer recommendations for exploring Ludlow and the surrounding area.

For those seeking a more rural retreat, The Bringewood Guest House offers a peaceful setting just outside of Ludlow. This traditional farmhouse B&B features comfortable rooms with countryside views, a delicious breakfast made with homemade and locally sourced ingredients, and a tranquil garden where guests can unwind and enjoy the picturesque surroundings.

In addition to these options, Ludlow also boasts several other bed and breakfast establishments that provide comfortable accommodation, personal service, and a homely atmosphere. These smaller properties are perfect for travellers looking for a more intimate and authentic experience during their stay in Ludlow. Whether it's a historic coaching inn, a modern boutique hotel, or a cosy bed and breakfast, Ludlow's accommodation options cater to a range of preferences and ensure that visitors have a delightful and memorable stay in this picturesque market town.

Self-Catering Options

Ludlow also offers a variety of self-catering accommodation options for visitors who prefer the flexibility and independence of their own space. One popular choice is The Old Bakehouse, a charming cottage located in the heart of Ludlow's historic town centre. This well-appointed property features a fully equipped kitchen, a cosy living area, and comfortable bedrooms, making it the perfect choice for families or small groups looking to enjoy a home-away-from-home experience.

Another self-catering option in Ludlow is The Coach House, a beautifully renovated property set within a private courtyard just a short walk from the town centre. This stylish and modern accommodation boasts a well-equipped kitchen, spacious living areas, and luxurious bedrooms, providing guests with all the comforts and amenities they need for a relaxing and enjoyable stay.

For those seeking a more rural retreat, Ludlow also offers a range of self-catering cottages and farmhouses in the surrounding countryside.

These properties provide guests with the opportunity to experience the tranquillity and natural beauty of the Shropshire countryside while still being within easy reach of Ludlow's attractions and amenities.

Whether it's a cosy cottage in the town centre or a secluded farmhouse in the countryside, Ludlow's self-catering options cater to a range of preferences and ensure that visitors have a comfortable and enjoyable stay in this picturesque market town.

Chapter Four: Dining and Cuisine

Traditional Ludlow Dishes

Ludlow is known for its traditional British cuisine, and there are several dishes that visitors must try when visiting the town. One of the most iconic dishes is the classic fish and chips. This dish typically consists of battered and deep-fried fish, such as cod or haddock, served with a side of thick-cut chips (fries) and mushy peas. The fish is often accompanied by tartar sauce or malt vinegar, and it is a beloved staple of British pub fare.

Another traditional Ludlow dish is the steak and ale pie. This hearty and comforting dish features tender chunks of beef cooked in a rich and savoury ale-based gravy, all encased in a flaky pastry crust. The pie is typically served with a side of mashed potatoes and seasonal vegetables, making it a satisfying and filling meal that is perfect for a cosy evening out.

On Sundays, visitors to Ludlow can also indulge in a traditional Sunday roast, which typically consists of roasted meat (such as beef, lamb, or chicken), served with roasted potatoes, Yorkshire pudding, seasonal vegetables, and gravy. This classic meal is a favourite among locals and visitors alike, and it is often enjoyed as a leisurely family meal in one of Ludlow's historic pubs or restaurants.

In addition to these classic dishes, Ludlow also offers a variety of other traditional British fare, such as bangers and mash (sausages and mashed potatoes), shepherd's pie (a savoury meat pie topped with mashed potatoes), and sticky toffee pudding (a moist sponge cake drizzled with toffee sauce). These dishes showcase the rich and comforting flavours of British cuisine, and they are a must-try for anyone looking to experience the culinary traditions of Ludlow.

Fine Dining Restaurants

Ludlow, known for its gastronomic excellence, boasts several fine dining establishments, each offering a unique culinary experience.

Mr. Underhill's:
Location: Nestled near Ludlow Castle, Mr. Underhill's is a Michelin-starred restaurant.
Cuisine: Specialising in modern British cuisine with a focus on locally sourced ingredients, the menu reflects a commitment to quality and creativity.

Drapers Hall Restaurant:
Location: Housed in a historic building, Drapers Hall Restaurant combines elegance with a sense of heritage.
Signature Dishes: Offers a seasonal menu featuring exquisite dishes crafted with precision, showcasing a blend of traditional and contemporary flavours.

The Church Inn (Fine Dining Section):
Location: Within The Church Inn, there is a fine dining section that elevates the culinary experience.
Ambiance: The intimate setting complements the carefully curated menu, which often includes dishes with a modern twist on classic British fare.

Forelles at Fishmore Hall:
Location: Situated just outside Ludlow, Forelles at Fishmore Hall provides a luxurious dining experience.
Setting: With a focus on refined dining, this restaurant offers a sophisticated atmosphere, complemented by panoramic views of the surrounding countryside.

La Bécasse:
Location: Tucked away on Corve Street, La Bécasse is celebrated for its French-inspired cuisine.
Chef's Specials: Known for its inventive tasting menus, the chef showcases culinary prowess through a selection of meticulously crafted dishes.

Overton Grange Hotel & Restaurant:

Location: A short drive from Ludlow, this restaurant within Overton Grange Hotel is a hidden treasure.

Gourmet Experience: Combining a charming setting with gourmet delights, it offers an extensive menu featuring locally sourced and seasonal ingredients.

Old Downton Lodge:

Location: Located in Ludlow's outskirts, Old Downton Lodge is renowned for its fine dining experience.

Fine Wine Selection: The restaurant complements its menu with an impressive wine list, enhancing the overall dining experience.

The Town House Ludlow:

Location: Centrally located, The Town House Ludlow offers an intimate dining setting.

Chef's Creations: Known for its chef's specials and carefully curated menus, this restaurant provides an elevated culinary journey.

These fine dining establishments in Ludlow showcase the town's commitment to culinary excellence, making it a destination for food enthusiasts seeking sophisticated and memorable dining experiences

Local Cafes and Pubs

Ludlow, a charming market town in England, boasts a variety of local cafes and pubs that cater to diverse tastes.

The Church Inn:
Location: Nestled near Ludlow Castle, The Church Inn offers a historic ambiance.
Specialty: Known for its traditional ales and hearty pub fare, it's a favourite among locals and visitors alike.

Café on the Square:
Location: Situated in Ludlow's central square, this café provides a perfect spot for people-watching.
Highlights: Serves freshly brewed coffee, artisanal pastries, and light lunches. The outdoor seating adds to the delightful experience.

The Feathers Hotel:

Location: A landmark in Ludlow, The Feathers Hotel combines a historic setting with a vibrant pub atmosphere.

Menu: Offers a diverse menu, including classic pub dishes and a wide selection of beverages. The Tudor-style architecture enhances the overall charm.

De Greys Tea Rooms:

Location: Tucked away on a quaint street, De Grey's exudes an old-world charm.

Specialty: Renowned for its afternoon teas, this establishment also serves homemade cakes and light lunches, creating a delightful vintage experience.

The Bull Hotel Bar:

Location: Adjacent to Ludlow's bustling market, The Bull Hotel Bar is a popular gathering spot.

Features: The bar showcases a selection of local ales and spirits, making it a great place to unwind after exploring Ludlow's attractions.

The Church Stretton Brewery Tap:

Location: A short drive from Ludlow, this brewery tap offers a rural escape.

Beer Selection: Known for its craft beers, visitors can enjoy freshly brewed options along with views of the surrounding countryside.

Castle Tea Rooms:
Location: Overlooking Ludlow Castle, this tea room provides a picturesque setting.
Menu: Serves traditional afternoon tea, light lunches, and a variety of teas, making it an ideal stop for those seeking a relaxed and scenic dining experience.

The Charlton Arms:
Location: Set along the River Teme, The Charlton Arms offers a riverside retreat.
Attractions: Besides the inviting pub atmosphere, visitors can enjoy the scenic riverside garden and a selection of classic pub dishes.
These establishments collectively contribute to Ludlow's vibrant culinary scene, offering a range of options for travellers seeking both traditional and contemporary dining experiences.

Ludlow is renowned for its dining and cuisine, making it a popular destination for food enthusiasts. The town is home to a variety of restaurants, cafes, and pubs, offering a diverse range of culinary experiences to suit all tastes and preferences.

One of Ludlow's main attractions is its vibrant food scene, with many establishments showcasing the best of local and seasonal produce. Visitors can indulge in traditional British cuisine at one of the town's historic pubs, where they can enjoy hearty meals such as fish and chips, steak and ale pie, and traditional Sunday roasts.

For those seeking a more upscale dining experience, Ludlow also offers a number of fine dining restaurants that showcase the talents of top chefs. These establishments often focus on modern British cuisine, with an emphasis on using locally sourced ingredients to create innovative and delicious dishes.

In addition to its restaurants and pubs, Ludlow is also home to a thriving market scene, with regular food markets offering a wide range of fresh produce, artisanal goods, and local delicacies. Visitors can sample and purchase a variety of cheeses, meats, breads, pastries, and other gourmet treats, making it the perfect place to stock up on picnic supplies or souvenirs to take home.

Overall, Ludlow's dining and cuisine scene is a major draw for visitors, offering a rich tapestry of culinary experiences that celebrate the best of local and regional flavours. Whether it's enjoying a leisurely meal at a cosy pub, indulging in fine dining at a top restaurant, or exploring the bustling food markets, visitors are sure to find something to tantalise their taste buds in this charming market town.

Chapter Five: Outdoor Activities

Hiking Trails

Ludlow, a charming town known for its picturesque landscapes, offers diverse hiking trails catering to various skill levels. The popular "Ludlow Loop" provides a moderate trek through lush forests and offers panoramic views of the surrounding mountains. For a more challenging experience, consider the "Peak Trail," leading to the summit with breathtaking vistas.

Nature enthusiasts may prefer the "Riverfront Trail," meandering along the Black River, providing opportunities for birdwatching and serene waterside strolls. Families can enjoy the "Family Adventure Trail," designed for all ages with informative markers and engaging activities along the way.

Remember to check local trail maps, adhere to safety guidelines, and explore Ludlow's hiking treasures like the Healdville Trail and Okemo State Forest for an unforgettable outdoor adventure.

Cycling Routes

Ludlow boasts scenic cycling routes, appealing to both casual riders and avid cyclists. The "Okemo Valley Loop" offers a moderate ride through rolling hills, passing by quaint villages and the picturesque Okemo Valley Golf Club. For a more challenging adventure, cyclists can tackle the "Okemo Mountain Ascent," a route leading up to Okemo's summit with rewarding views of the Green Mountains.

Exploring the "Ludlow Lakes Region Trail" takes riders around shimmering lakes and through wooded areas, providing a refreshing mix of nature and tranquillity. Families can enjoy the "Black River Bikeway," a leisurely path along the river, suitable for all skill levels.

Ensure a safe and enjoyable ride by checking local cycling maps, following traffic rules, and exploring Ludlow's diverse landscapes on two wheels. Don't forget to take breaks at local cafes or parks to savour the charm of Ludlow during your cycling adventure.

Parks and Gardens

Ludlow boasts a variety of parks and gardens, each offering a unique blend of natural beauty and recreational opportunities. Start your exploration with the "Dorsey Park," a family-friendly destination featuring playgrounds, picnic areas, and sports facilities. For a serene experience, visit the "Buttermilk Falls and Crispin's Crispianus Park," where cascading waterfalls and walking trails provide a peaceful escape.

Nature enthusiasts will appreciate the "Okemo State Forest," offering hiking trails, fishing spots, and a chance to immerse in Ludlow's wilderness. The "Jackson Gore Village Green" is a charming public space, hosting events and providing a relaxing setting with well-maintained greenery.

Garden enthusiasts can explore "The Green Mountain Gardeners' Demonstration Garden," showcasing local flora and offering gardening inspiration. Additionally, Ludlow's "Fletcher Farm School for the Arts and Crafts" features lovely gardens surrounding historic buildings, providing a cultural and natural retreat.

Whether you seek recreation or relaxation, Ludlow's parks and gardens provide a delightful blend of outdoor experiences, making your visit a memorable one.

Ludlow offers a diverse range of outdoor activities, catering to nature lovers and adventure seekers alike. Begin your exploration with hiking, as Ludlow boasts numerous trails such as the "Ludlow Loop" and "Peak Trail," each providing varying levels of difficulty and stunning views of the surrounding mountains.

Cycling enthusiasts can pedal through picturesque landscapes with routes like the "Okemo Valley Loop" and the challenging "Okemo Mountain Ascent," while families may prefer the leisurely "Black River Bikeway" or the scenic "Ludlow Lakes Region Trail."

For those seeking tranquillity, parks like "Dorsey Park" and the "Buttermilk Falls and Crispin's Crispianus Park" offer green spaces, playgrounds, and walking trails. Nature lovers can immerse themselves in the pristine surroundings of the "Okemo State Forest," providing hiking trails and fishing spots.

Garden enthusiasts will appreciate Ludlow's "Green Mountain Gardeners' Demonstration Garden" and the charming gardens surrounding the historic buildings at the "Fletcher Farm School for the Arts and Crafts."

Whether hiking, cycling, or enjoying the parks and gardens, Ludlow's outdoor activities promise a blend of adventure, relaxation, and natural beauty for a truly memorable experience

Chapter Six: Cultural Experiences

Ludlow Arts and Crafts

Ludlow, is home to a vibrant Arts and Crafts scene. The Ludlow Arts and Crafts movement encompasses a diverse range of artistic endeavours, including traditional crafts, visual arts, and performances.

Local artisans and craftsmen play a pivotal role in preserving and promoting the Arts and Crafts heritage in Ludlow. Visitors can explore charming galleries showcasing handmade ceramics, textiles, and intricate woodwork, reflecting the principles of the Arts and Crafts movement that emerged in the late 19th century.

One notable venue is the Ludlow Assembly Rooms, a cultural hub hosting various artistic events, exhibitions, and workshops. Here, one can witness live performances, engage with local artists, and gain insight into the rich cultural tapestry of Ludlow.

The Ludlow Arts and Crafts Festival, held annually, attracts artists and enthusiasts from far and wide. This event provides a platform for local talent to exhibit their creations and fosters a sense of community through shared appreciation for craftsmanship.

The town's architecture also echoes the Arts and Crafts ethos, with buildings adorned with intricate detailing and a commitment to craftsmanship. Ludlow Castle, a prominent landmark, stands as a testament to the town's historical and artistic significance.

In Ludlow, the Arts and Crafts movement isn't just a historical relic but a living tradition. It weaves itself into the fabric of daily life, creating a unique and vibrant cultural experience for both residents and visitors alike.

Festivals and Events

Ludlow hosts a diverse array of festivals and events throughout the year, creating a lively and engaging atmosphere for both locals and visitors. Here are some notable celebrations in Ludlow:

Ludlow Food Festival: A highlight for food enthusiasts, this festival showcases the region's culinary delights. Local and international chefs come together to celebrate the finest produce, offering tastings, demonstrations, and opportunities to indulge in gourmet delights.

Ludlow Arts Festival: Celebrating the town's artistic spirit, this event features a range of visual arts, performances, and workshops. Attendees can immerse themselves in the local art scene, discovering talent from various mediums and enjoying the vibrant cultural offerings.

Ludlow Medieval Christmas Fayre: Transporting visitors back in time, this festive event transforms Ludlow into a mediaeval wonderland. With period costumes, traditional crafts, and festive entertainment, it offers a unique and enchanting experience for families and history enthusiasts alike.

Ludlow Fringe Festival: This multi-disciplinary arts festival brings together performers, artists, and creatives to showcase their talents. The program includes live music, theatre, comedy, and other performances, providing a platform for both established and emerging artists.

Ludlow Green Festival: Focused on sustainability and environmental awareness, this festival promotes green living and eco-friendly practices. It features workshops, exhibitions, and activities that encourage a deeper understanding of environmental issues and inspire positive change.

Ludlow Marches Beer and Food Festival: A treat for beer and food aficionados, this festival celebrates the region's diverse offerings. Breweries and food producers showcase their creations, allowing attendees to savour a wide variety of local flavours.

These festivals not only contribute to Ludlow's cultural richness but also serve as a testament to the town's commitment to community engagement and celebration of its heritage. Whether you're interested in culinary delights, the arts, or historical reimaginings, Ludlow's festival calendar has something to offer for everyone.

Local Markets

Ludlow boasts a vibrant market scene that adds to the town's charm and provides a unique shopping experience. Here are some of the local markets that contribute to Ludlow's lively atmosphere:

Ludlow Market: The traditional Ludlow market is held in the town centre multiple times a week, showcasing a wide array of goods. From fresh produce and local delicacies to handmade crafts and antiques, Ludlow Market offers a diverse range of products. It's a perfect place to explore and discover local treasures.

Ludlow Farmers' Market: Celebrating the region's agricultural richness, the Ludlow Farmers' Market is a must-visit for those seeking fresh, locally sourced produce. Held regularly, it features farmers, growers, and artisan food producers, allowing visitors to connect directly with the people behind the products.

Ludlow Antique Market: For enthusiasts of vintage and antique finds, Ludlow's antique market is a treasure trove. Stroll through stalls filled with unique items, from furniture and collectibles to vintage clothing. It's a great place for collectors and those looking to add a touch of history to their homes.

Ludlow Arts and Crafts Market: Embracing the town's artistic spirit, this market showcases handmade crafts, artworks, and unique creations by local artists and artisans. It provides a platform for creators to share their talents and offers visitors the opportunity to acquire one-of-a-kind pieces.

Ludlow Christmas Market: During the festive season, Ludlow transforms into a winter wonderland with its Christmas market. The streets are adorned with lights, and stalls offer festive treats, handmade gifts, and a joyful atmosphere. It's a perfect place to experience the magic of the holidays.

Visiting these markets not only provides a chance to shop for unique items but also allows visitors to immerse themselves in Ludlow's local culture and community spirit. Whether you're a foodie, an art enthusiast, or someone who enjoys exploring markets, Ludlow's diverse market scene has something for everyone.

Chapter Seven: Day Trips

Nearby Towns and Villages

Ludlow offers a range of nearby towns and villages that are worth exploring. Here are some options:

Leominster: Located to the east of Ludlow, Leominster is known for its mediaeval architecture and antique shops. The town is surrounded by picturesque countryside, making it a pleasant destination for a day trip.

Bridgnorth: To the south-east of Ludlow, Bridgnorth is a market town divided into High Town and Low Town by the River Severn. The Severn Valley Railway and the historic funicular railway are notable attractions.

Knighton: Situated to the west of Ludlow, Knighton straddles the English-Welsh border. It's known for the Offa's Dyke Path and the beautiful countryside of the Marches.

Clun: Nestled in the Clun Valley, this tranquil village lies to the north-west of Ludlow. Clun

Castle and the surrounding hills make it an ideal spot for nature lovers and history enthusiasts.

Tenbury Wells: Positioned to the north-east, Tenbury Wells is renowned for its horticultural heritage and the annual Applefest. The Teme River adds charm to this market town.

Stokesay: While not a town, Stokesay is a nearby village famous for Stokesay Castle, a mediaeval manor house with stunning timber-framed architecture. It's a short drive from Ludlow and offers a glimpse into mediaeval life.

Cleobury Mortimer: Located to the east, this market town boasts timber-framed buildings and a lively atmosphere. The River Rea flows through, and the town is surrounded by scenic countryside.

When travelling between Ludlow and these destinations, consider the picturesque countryside routes, offering scenic views of the Shropshire Hills and the Welsh Marches. Whether you're interested in history, nature, or simply exploring charming market towns,

Ludlow's proximity to these destinations provides a diverse range of experiences.

Natural Landmarks

Ludlow and its surrounding areas are blessed with natural landmarks that showcase the beauty of the Shropshire countryside. Here are some notable natural attractions in Ludlow:

The Clee Hills: Dominating the skyline to the northeast of Ludlow, the Clee Hills offer breathtaking panoramic views of the surrounding landscape. Topped by Brown Clee Hill, the highest point in Shropshire, and Titterstone Clee Hill, these hills are perfect for hiking and provide a serene escape into nature.

Mortimer Forest: Located just to the northwest of Ludlow, Mortimer Forest is a haven for outdoor enthusiasts. It offers a variety of walking and cycling trails amidst ancient woodlands. High Vinnalls, the highest point in the forest, rewards hikers with stunning vistas.

The River Teme: Flowing through Ludlow, the River Teme adds charm to the town's landscape.

Stroll along the riverside, enjoy the scenic views, or perhaps partake in activities like fishing. The Ludlow Riverside Walk provides a delightful way to explore the riverbanks.

Dinham Bridge and Meadows: Crossing the River Teme, Dinham Bridge connects Ludlow to Dinham and provides a picturesque setting. The adjacent meadows are ideal for a leisurely walk, picnics, or simply enjoying the tranquil surroundings.

Ludlow Castle Gardens: While Ludlow Castle is a historic landmark, its gardens contribute to Ludlow's natural beauty. Explore the castle grounds, including the beautiful gardens with well-maintained lawns and scenic views of the surrounding hills.

Shropshire Hills Area of Outstanding Natural Beauty (AONB): Ludlow is situated within the Shropshire Hills AONB, ensuring that natural beauty surrounds the town. The undulating hills, valleys, and diverse flora and fauna make this area a haven for those seeking a connection with nature.

Bringewood and Titterstone Clee Hill Geopark: Ludlow and its surroundings are part of the Geopark, showcasing geological features such as rocky outcrops and ancient landscapes. Titterstone Clee Hill is especially known for its geological significance.

Exploring Ludlow's natural landmarks offers a harmonious blend of history, culture, and the great outdoors. Whether you prefer scenic walks, panoramic views, or riverside strolls, Ludlow provides a diverse range of natural attractions for nature enthusiasts.

Embarking on day trips from Ludlow unveils a tapestry of historical, cultural, and scenic wonders that enrich the traveller's experience. Here's a glimpse into the possibilities:

The journey to Leominster, positioned to the east of Ludlow, unfolds in a charming mediaeval town adorned with antique shops. Stroll through its historical streets and immerse yourself in the quaint ambiance.

Venturing southeast leads to Bridgnorth, a town divided into High Town and Low Town by the

River Severn. Explore the Severn Valley Railway, historic funicular railway, and relish the unique charm of this riverside locale.

To the west lies Knighton, a town straddling the English-Welsh border. Discover the Offa's Dyke Path, providing panoramic views of the surrounding Marches countryside.

Heading northwest, one encounters Club, a tranquil village nestled in the Clun Valley. Clun Castle and the picturesque landscapes offer a serene retreat for history and nature enthusiasts alike.

Journeying northeast brings you to Tenbury Wells, renowned for its horticultural heritage and the annual Applefest. The Teme River meanders through, enhancing the town's idyllic charm.

While not a town, Stokesay beckons with its mediaeval manor house, Stokesay Castle. The timber-framed architecture and surrounding gardens provide a glimpse into a bygone era.

To the east lies Cleobury Mortimer, a market town adorned with timber-framed buildings. The River Rea flows through, and the town's lively atmosphere makes it a delightful stop.

Amidst Ludlow's natural treasures, the Clee Hills captivate with their panoramic views. Hike through ancient woodlands in Mortimer Forest, or enjoy the tranquillity of the River Teme along Ludlow's riverside.

Dinham Bridge and Meadows offer a picturesque escape, connecting Ludlow to the charming village of Dinham. The meadows provide an ideal setting for a leisurely walk or a relaxing picnic.

Ludlow Castle Gardens invite exploration within the town itself. Wander through the well-maintained lawns, enjoy the historic ambiance, and savour views of the surrounding hills.

Situated within the Shropshire Hills Area of Outstanding Natural Beauty (AONB), Ludlow opens the door to the breathtaking landscapes of the Shropshire Hills. A drive through this undulating terrain reveals the region's diverse flora and fauna.

As Ludlow and its surroundings unfold, each day trip promises a unique blend of history, culture, and natural beauty, ensuring a memorable and enriching experience for every traveller

Chapter Eight: Tips for Travelers

Packing Tips

Ludlow, with its charming streets and historical sites, is a fantastic destination. Here are some packing tips for a trip to Ludlow:

Weather-Appropriate Clothing:
Ludlow experiences a temperate climate, so pack layers. Bring comfortable walking shoes for exploring the cobbled streets and perhaps a light jacket, especially if you're visiting during the cooler months.

Electronics and Chargers:
Don't forget your camera or smartphone to capture Ludlow's picturesque landscapes and architecture. Remember to pack chargers and perhaps a power bank for those long days of exploration.

Travel Adapters:
If you're visiting from abroad, ensure you have the right travel adapters to charge your devices and plug into local outlets.

Guidebook or Maps:

Ludlow is rich in history, and having a guidebook or map can enhance your experience, to help navigate the town and learn more about its heritage.

Reusable Water Bottle:

Stay hydrated while exploring Ludlow. Bring a reusable water bottle to refill throughout the day, especially if you plan on walking and exploring the town on foot.

Snacks:

Pack some light snacks for energy during your excursions. This is particularly useful if you plan on spending a lot of time outdoors or exploring Ludlow's countryside.

Medication and First Aid Kit:

Pack any necessary medication and a basic first aid kit. While Ludlow has amenities, it's always good to be prepared for minor health issues or unexpected situations.

Local Currency:

Although credit cards are widely accepted, having some local currency can be useful, especially in smaller shops or markets.

Daypack or Tote Bag:
Bring a small daypack or tote bag for your daily explorations. It's handy for carrying essentials and any souvenirs you may pick up during your visit.

Travel Insurance Information:
Ensure you have your travel insurance information easily accessible. It's a good idea to be ready for unexpected situations.

Remember, Ludlow is a town with a rich history and unique charm, so be sure to pack in a way that allows you to fully immerse yourself in its cultural offerings. Whether you're strolling through Ludlow Castle, enjoying local cuisine, or browsing the vibrant markets, these packing tips should help you make the most of your Ludlow travel experience. Safe travels.

Language Basics

Ludlow is predominantly an English-speaking town, understanding some language basics can enhance your travel experience:

English Language:
English is the primary language spoken in Ludlow. Most locals and service providers communicate fluently in English, making it easy for travellers to navigate and interact.

Local Dialect:
Ludlow may have some local dialects or accents, but they are generally variations of standard English. Engaging with locals and immersing yourself in conversations can give you a feel for any unique linguistic nuances.

Politeness and Courtesy:
British culture places a strong emphasis on politeness. Saying "please" and "thank you" is customary, and addressing people with appropriate titles like "sir" or "ma'am" is considered polite.

Currency Terminology:

Familiarise yourself with basic currency terminology. The official currency is the British Pound (£), and understanding terms like "quid" for pounds and "pence" for the subunit will be helpful during transactions.

Common Phrases:
Knowing a few common phrases can help a lot. Basics like greetings ("hello," "good morning," "good evening"), asking for directions, and ordering food will make your interactions smoother.

Numbers and Measurements:
Understanding numbers and measurements in the metric system is useful. Road signs, distances, and some local information may be presented using metric units.

Local Attractions and Landmarks:
Knowing the names and pronunciation of key local attractions and landmarks can help you communicate effectively and seek directions from locals.

Emergency Phrases:

While it's unlikely you'll encounter any emergencies, being familiar with basic emergency phrases like "help," "police," and "hospital" is a good precaution.

Cultural Etiquette:
Understanding cultural norms and etiquettes related to language use is essential. For example, queueing (waiting in line) is a common practice, and maintaining a respectful distance when conversing is appreciated.

Language Apps:
Consider using language learning apps to quickly grasp essential phrases. Although English is widely spoken, locals often appreciate the effort to learn a bit of their language.

By embracing the language basics in Ludlow, you'll not only navigate the town more smoothly but also engage more authentically with its welcoming community.

Sustainable Travel Practices

Ludlow, with its rich history and picturesque landscapes, offers an opportunity to engage in sustainable travel practices. Here's a guide to promoting eco-friendly and responsible tourism in Ludlow:

Public Transportation:

Opt for public transportation or eco-friendly modes of travel to reach Ludlow. Once there, explore the town on foot or rent a bicycle to minimise your carbon footprint.

Accommodations:

Choose accommodations that prioritise sustainability. Look for hotels, bed and breakfasts, or guesthouses that have eco-friendly certifications, use renewable energy, and implement water-saving measures.

Waste Reduction:

Be mindful of waste. Use a water bottle that can be reused, use a coffee cup that can be refilled, and bring a shopping bag that can be reused. Ludlow has a strong focus on environmental conservation, and reducing single-use plastic helps contribute to this effort.

Support Local Businesses:
Opt to support local businesses and artisans. Purchasing locally-produced goods not only reduces your ecological impact but also contributes to the economic sustainability of the community.

Respect Natural Spaces:
Ludlow is surrounded by beautiful countryside. When exploring nature reserves, parks, or walking trails, follow designated paths, avoid littering, and respect wildlife habitats.

Culinary Choices:
Choose restaurants that emphasise locally-sourced, seasonal ingredients. This not only supports local farmers but also reduces the environmental impact associated with long-distance food transportation.

Cultural Sensitivity:
Respect the local culture and traditions. Ludlow has a strong sense of community, and being

culturally sensitive contributes to a positive and sustainable travel experience.

Educational Tours:
Engage in educational tours that promote environmental awareness. Ludlow Castle, for instance, often offers guided tours that delve into the historical and environmental aspects of the region.

Energy Conservation:
Practice energy conservation in your accommodations. Turn off lights and electronic devices when not in use, and be mindful of water usage.

Leave No Trace:
Whether you're exploring Ludlow's historic sites or enjoying its natural beauty, follow the "Leave No Trace" principles. Minimise your impact on the environment and leave cultural and natural sites as you found them.

By incorporating these sustainable travel practices, you can enjoy Ludlow's charm while contributing to the preservation of its cultural and natural heritage. Responsible tourism ensures that future generations can also experience the beauty that Ludlow has to offer.

Chapter Nine: Sample Itineraries

One Day in Ludlow

England's charming market town in Shropshire. With its picturesque streets, historic buildings, and stunning countryside, it's a wonderful destination for a day trip or a weekend getaway. As a conscious traveller, it's important to consider the environmental impact of your visit. Here's a sustainable travel guide for spending one day in Ludlow.

Morning:

Start your day with a leisurely stroll through Ludlow's vibrant market. Here, you'll find an array of locally sourced produce, artisan crafts, and delicious food. Be sure to bring along your reusable shopping bag to reduce the need for single-use plastic bags. Support local farmers and artisans by purchasing fresh fruits, vegetables, and handmade goods.

After exploring the market, head to a local café for a morning pick-me-up. Bring along your refillable coffee cup to enjoy your beverage without contributing to the waste generated by disposable coffee cups. Many cafés in Ludlow are committed to sustainability and are happy to fill up your reusable cup.

Midday:

Ludlow is home to several beautiful parks and gardens, perfect for a midday picnic. Pack a lunch using the fresh ingredients you purchased at the market and bring along your reusable water bottle to stay hydrated. Enjoy a peaceful afternoon surrounded by nature, taking in the beauty of Ludlow's green spaces.

Afternoon:

In the afternoon, take a guided walking tour of Ludlow to learn about its rich history and architecture. Many tour operators in Ludlow prioritise sustainable practices, such as walking tours that minimise the use of fossil fuels. By choosing a guided walking tour, you can explore the town while reducing your carbon footprint.

Evening:

As the day comes to a close, treat yourself to a delicious meal at one of Ludlow's many restaurants. Look for establishments that prioritise local and organic ingredients, as well as those that support sustainable fishing and farming practices. By dining at a sustainable restaurant, you can enjoy a meal that is not only delicious but also environmentally friendly.

Before heading home, take some time to reflect on your day in Ludlow. By incorporating sustainable practices into your visit, you've made a positive impact on the local community and environment. As you travel back home, remember to pack up your reusable items and dispose of any waste responsibly.

In conclusion, spending one day in Ludlow can be both enjoyable and sustainable. By bringing along your reusable water bottle, refillable coffee cup, and reusable shopping bag, you can minimise your environmental impact while supporting local businesses and enjoying all that Ludlow has to offer.

Weekend Getaway Itinerary

A weekend getaway in Ludlow offers the perfect opportunity to immerse yourself in the town's rich history, stunning countryside, and vibrant local culture. Here's a detailed itinerary for a sustainable weekend getaway in Ludlow:

Day 1:

Morning:

Arrive in Ludlow and check into your accommodation. Look for eco-friendly hotels, bed and breakfasts, or guesthouses that prioritise sustainability and environmental responsibility.

After settling in, start your day with a visit to Ludlow's bustling market. Spend some time exploring the stalls and supporting local farmers and artisans by purchasing fresh produce, handmade crafts, and locally sourced goods. Remember to bring along your reusable shopping bag to minimise waste.

Midday:

For lunch, head to a local café or deli that offers organic, locally sourced options. Enjoy a delicious meal made with fresh ingredients while supporting sustainable farming practices.

Afternoon:

In the afternoon, take a leisurely walk through Ludlow's beautiful parks and gardens. Pack a picnic using the items you purchased at the market and enjoy a relaxing afternoon surrounded by nature.

Evening:

For dinner, choose a restaurant that prioritises sustainability and supports local farmers and producers. Indulge in a meal made with organic, seasonal ingredients and enjoy the vibrant culinary scene that Ludlow has to offer.

Day 2:

Morning:

Start your day with a guided walking tour of Ludlow to learn about the town's fascinating history and architecture. Many tour operators in Ludlow offer sustainable walking tours that minimise the use of fossil fuels, allowing you to explore the town while reducing your carbon footprint.

Midday:

After the walking tour, take some time to visit Ludlow Castle, a historic landmark that offers stunning views of the surrounding countryside. Learn about the castle's history and its significance to the town while appreciating its architectural beauty.

Afternoon:

In the afternoon, consider taking a nature walk or hike in the countryside surrounding Ludlow. There are several scenic trails and paths that offer breathtaking views and opportunities to connect with nature.

Evening:

As your weekend getaway comes to a close, reflect on your time in Ludlow and consider how you can continue to incorporate sustainable practices into your travels. Before leaving, be sure to dispose of any waste responsibly and pack up your reusable items for the journey home.

By following this itinerary for a sustainable weekend getaway in Ludlow, you can enjoy all that the town has to offer while minimising your environmental impact and supporting local businesses and initiatives.

Family-Friendly Plan

Ludlow offers a variety of family-friendly activities and attractions, making it the perfect destination for a fun and memorable getaway with the kids. Here's a detailed plan for a family-friendly trip to Ludlow:

Day 1:

Morning:

Arrive in Ludlow and check into your family-friendly accommodation. Look for hotels, bed and breakfasts, or vacation rentals that cater to families, offering amenities such as spacious rooms, play areas, and child-friendly facilities.

After settling in, start your day with a visit to Ludlow's market. Explore the stalls with the kids and let them pick out some fresh produce, local treats, or handmade crafts to enjoy during your stay.

Midday:

For lunch, head to a family-friendly café or restaurant that offers a children's menu and a relaxed atmosphere. Enjoy a meal together and fuel up for the day's adventures.

Afternoon:

In the afternoon, take the family to Ludlow Castle for a guided tour. Learn about the castle's history and explore its grounds while enjoying the stunning views of the surrounding countryside.

Evening:

For dinner, choose a restaurant that welcomes families and offers a kid-friendly menu. Enjoy a delicious meal together and soak in the vibrant atmosphere of Ludlow's culinary scene.

Day 2:

Morning:

Start your day with a visit to one of Ludlow's family-friendly attractions, such as the Ludlow Museum or the Ludlow Food Centre. Both offer educational and interactive experiences that are perfect for kids of all ages.

Midday:

After exploring the town, consider taking a nature walk or hike in the countryside surrounding Ludlow. There are several family-friendly trails and paths that offer opportunities for outdoor exploration and adventure.

Afternoon:

In the afternoon, visit one of Ludlow's parks or gardens for some outdoor playtime. Let the kids run around, play games, or have a picnic in the beautiful natural surroundings.

Evening:

As your family-friendly weekend getaway comes to an end, reflect on your time in Ludlow and consider how you can continue to create fun and memorable experiences with your family. Before leaving, be sure to tidy up any messes and pack up your belongings for the journey home.

By following this family-friendly plan for a trip to Ludlow, you can create lasting memories with your loved ones while enjoying all that the town has to offer.

Conclusion and Final Tips for a Memorable Trip

As you prepare for your trip to Ludlow, it's important to keep a few final tips in mind to ensure a memorable and enjoyable visit.

First and foremost, be sure to take the time to explore the town's rich history. Ludlow Castle is a must-see attraction, offering a fascinating glimpse into the area's mediaeval past. Take a guided tour to learn more about the castle's storied history and enjoy the stunning views from the top of the tower.

In addition to the castle, be sure to wander through Ludlow's charming streets, taking in the historic architecture and quaint shops and cafes. The town's market is also a great place to pick up some local goods and souvenirs.

Food lovers will find plenty to delight their taste buds in Ludlow, with its thriving food scene and numerous award-winning restaurants. Be sure to sample some of the local specialties, such as traditional Shropshire fare and artisanal cheeses.

For those who enjoy outdoor activities, Ludlow's surrounding countryside offers ample opportunities for hiking, cycling, and exploring the natural beauty of the area. Consider taking a leisurely stroll along the River Teme or embarking on a more challenging hike in the nearby Shropshire Hills.

Finally, be sure to take advantage of any events or festivals taking place during your visit. Ludlow hosts a number of cultural events throughout the year, including food festivals, music concerts, and historical reenactments.

With these final tips in mind, you're sure to have a memorable and enjoyable trip to Ludlow. So pack your bags, prepare for adventure, and get ready to explore all that this charming town has to offer. Happy travels.

Printed in Great Britain
by Amazon

37339586R00056